BABY SEEDS TO BIG PLANTS
Botany for Kids
Nature for Children Edition

SPEEDY
PUBLISHING

Speedy Publishing LLC
40 E. Main St. #1156
Newark, DE 19711
www.speedypublishing.com

Most plants grow

from seeds.

A seed is an embryonic plant enclosed in a protective outer covering known as the seed coat.

There are
two groups
os seeds, the
angiosperms and
gymnosperms.

Angiosperms are the flowering plants and gymnosperms do not have flowers or ovaries.

Within each seed lives a tiny plant, called an embryo.

With the right amount of water, oxygen and temperature this embryo will come out of the seed and begin its life.

There are over 200,000 identified plant species and the list is growing all the time.

While using energy from sunlight, plants turn carbon dioxide into food in a process called photosynthesis.

Plants use
water to carry
moisture and
nutrients back
and forth
between the
roots and leaves.

In the agricultural industry, to ensure crops of food grow well water is often added to soil in the form of irrigation.

Fertilizer also
provides plants
with nutrients
and is usually
given to plants
when watering.

Plants reproduce more plants through flowers. The flowers have pollen. When the pollen spreads to other plants, it produces fruit and seeds.

Bees or the
wind pollinate
most plants.

Their leaves
have a
substance called
chlorophyll
which changes
energy from the
sun into food.

Plant roots grow underground and are not seen. Roots help to hold the plant up and bring in food and water from the soil.

The Conifers are cone-bearing seed plants. Most of them are trees. Trees grow taller by growth from new cells at the tips of their branches.

Species of conifers can be found in almost all parts of the world.

Fern is a vascular, seedless plant. They live in shady places that provide enough moisture, such as forests, fields, swamps and areas near the streams.

Mosses are tiny plants. Most mosses can reach 0.4 to 4 inches in height. A patch of moss is made of many tiny moss plants packed together so that they can hold water for as long as possible.